Front Cover: "Torn Building Towers" by Wally Gilbert, 2016.

Back Cover: "High Water – New York" by Wally Gilbert, 2016.

Towers

by

Wally Gilbert

Copyright Notice: Copyright ©2017 by Wally Gilbert

An Exhibition

at

Viridian Artists

October 3rd – October 28th, 2017

Opening Reception:
Thursday, October 5th, 6 to 8PM

548 West 28th Street, #632
Chelsea, NY 10001

Tuesday – Saturday: 12 – 6PM

Gallery Statement:

Viridian Artists Inc. is pleased to present an exhibition of digital imagery by the artist/scientist/photographer Wally Gilbert, entitled "Towers".

Wally Gilbert has always been modest about his achievements.

If you looked him up on Wikipedia (https://en.wikipedia.org/wiki/Walter_Gilbert) , you would learn that he is not only a Nobel Prize-winning scientist but also a Cambridge graduate, a Harvard professor, and a noted and honored expert in numerous other scientific investigations. But after retiring from Harvard in 2001, he turned to the artistic side of his brain and began a career in digital photography, transforming his images with Photoshop and undoubtedly other self-invented techniques to make fascinating compositions suggestive of depths beyond reality.

Gilbert has been working with digital photography now for over a decade, sometimes exploring color, sometimes focusing on black & white imagery. In this exhibit, his focus is on color and light which he investigates and manipulates, transforming fragments of photographs into a plethora of artistic and arresting abstract and sometimes nearly realistic artworks.

The artist/scientist continues his exploration of the digital media of photography, approaching it with scientific gusto, artistic freedom and the wisdom of experimentation, pushing and transforming his images by taking color to the extreme. The work in his latest exhibition begins with color, light and overlapping shapes, creating complex abstractions that leave the viewer to imagine their origins. This time, many of the images begin with towering architectonic structures, perhaps reminding us - with the title "Torn Building Towers"- of The Twin Towers of 9/11.

Gilbert explores the medium of photography zealously, searching for beauty and then translating that beauty into his own imagistic language of color and form. He first captures photographically a wide variety of subjects, translating the subjects into artistic images that he enhances digitally, pushing colors and shapes creatively and scientifically perhaps, reminding us that the thinking processes of artists and scientists are more alike than we previously realized.

With this new series of images, Gilbert continues exploring architectural imagery, but now repeating & altering it so that the images dance before your eyes. They glow with color driven to full saturation creating new interactions, until they have become "abstract meditations" at times approaching the psychedelic images of the 70's. A time so different from now but perhaps not so for the show at the Whitney of 70's Political Art which featured the works of many old friends.

"In his digitally altered photographs, Wally Gilbert slices up and weaves city scenes, cranking color values off the charts. Ember red burns against royal purple, and lemon-yellow pops against red and violet, in "Torn Building Tower – Triptych." Zing! The three narrow vertical panels echo forms of the buildings they depict, which tumble, fold, and open into dazzling, game-board grids."
-- Cate McQuaid, Boston Globe, March 31, 2017

His art was featured in the Saatchi Fair in London in September in this year as well as numerous venues on the East & West Coast of the US. We hope that you will be able to meet this outstanding artist and share his vision through seeing these incredibly fascinating artworks.

Vernita Nemec   Chelsea, New York

Catalogue of Images

Torn Building Towers	10
Youth Day – Krakow	11
Mysterious Towers	12
Doors to Nowhere	13
Torn Building #2 – Red	14
Old Car Diptych	15
Broken City	16
Broken City #II	17
Multiply Diptych	18
Tall Red	19
Bewildered	20
Wiggle Triptych	21
Windows Diptych #1	22
Windows Diptych #2	23
High Water – New York	24
Torment	25
Sails	26
Sails #2 - Yellow	27
Sails #2 - Red	28

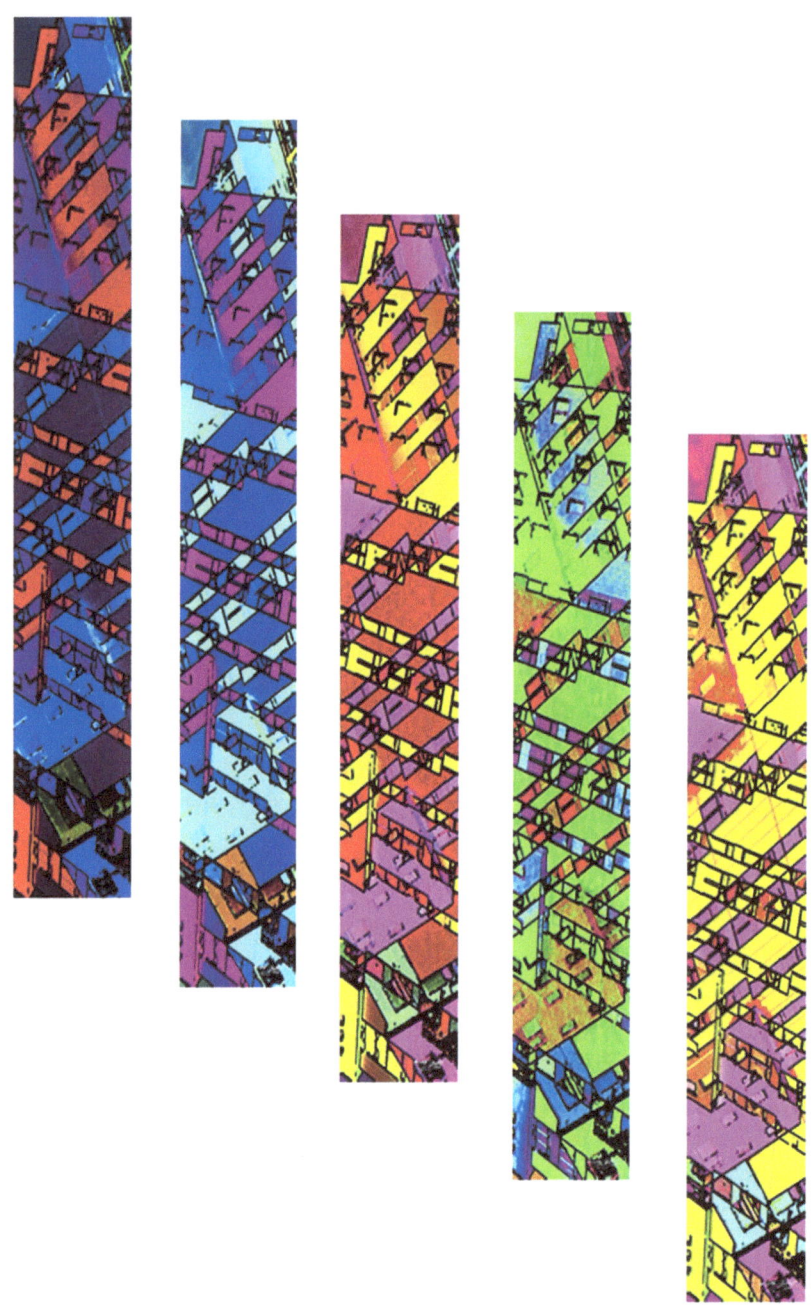

Torn Building Towers

2016, Five Panels, each 72" x 10",
Printed on Aluminum, edition of 5.

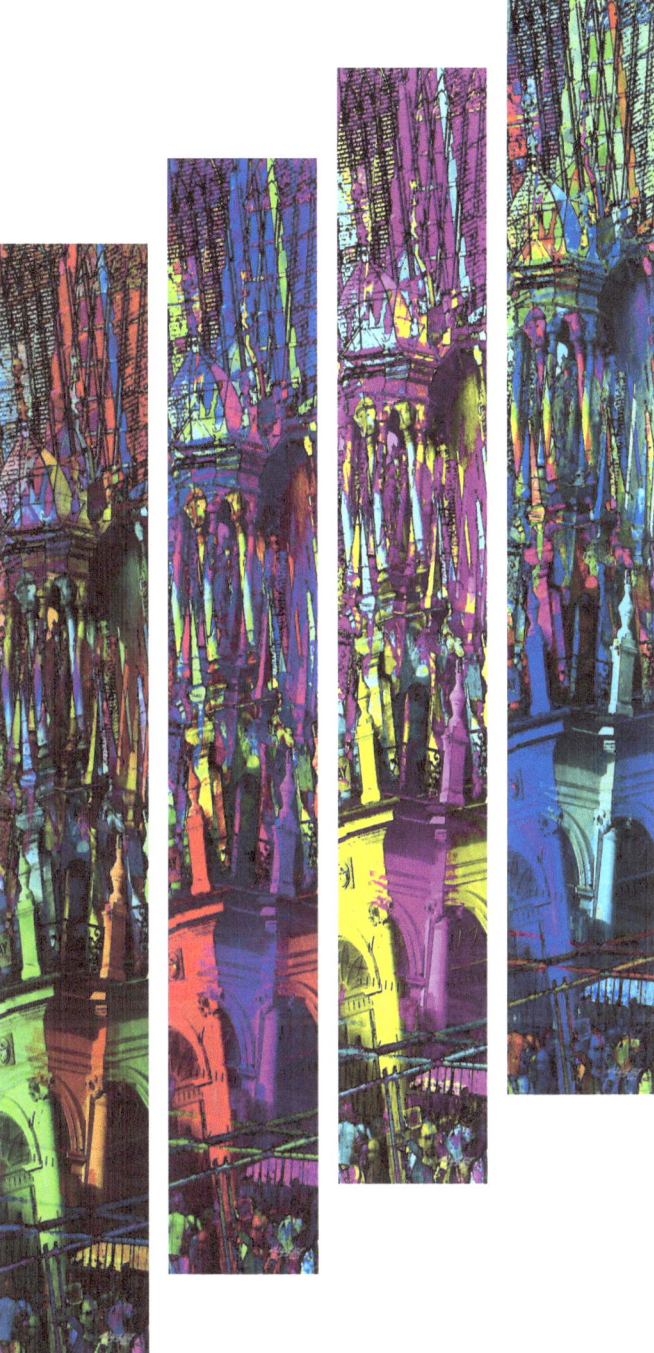

Youth Day – Krakow

2016, Four Panels, each 72" x 10",
Printed on Aluminum, edition of 5.

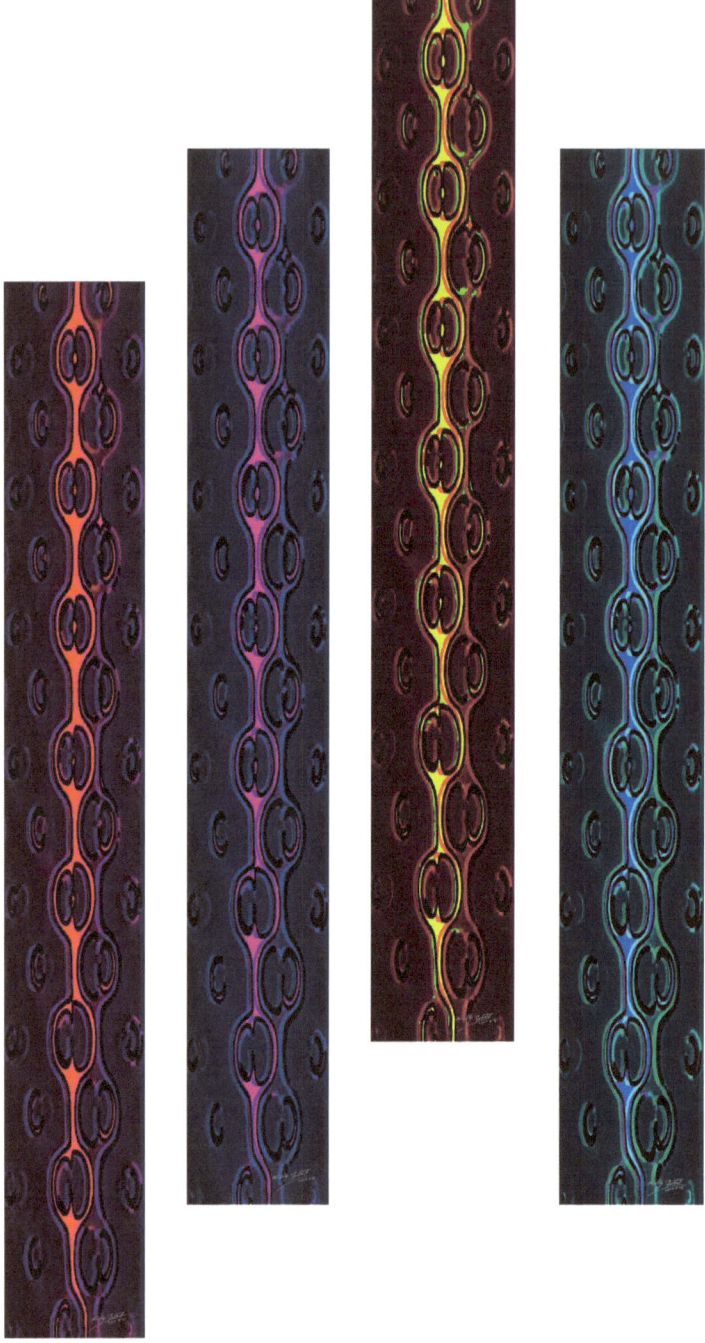

Mysterious Towers

2017, Four Panels, each 72" x 10",
Printed on Aluminum, edition of 5

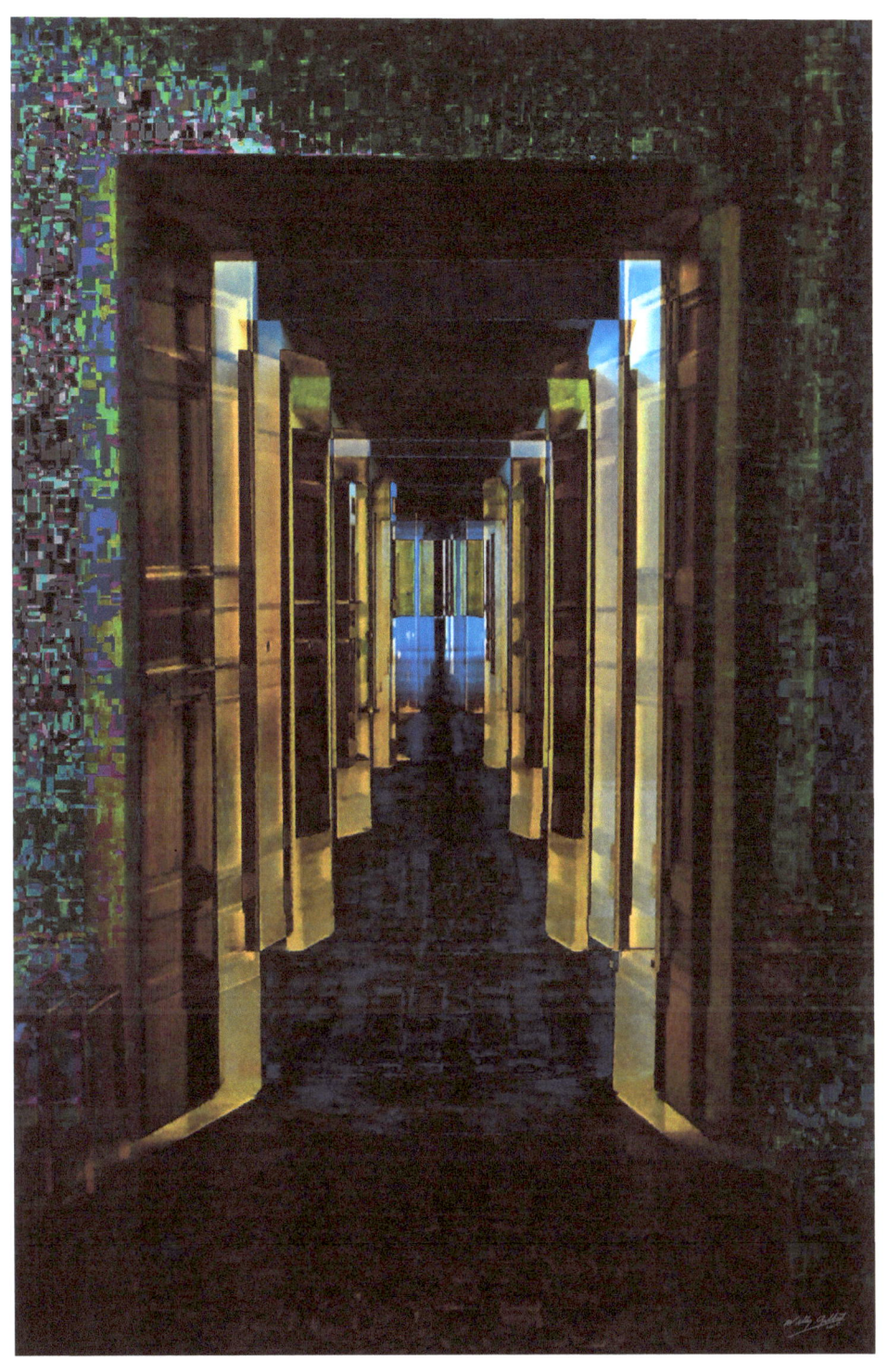

Doors to Nowhere

2015, 60" x 40",
Printed on Aluminum, edition of 5

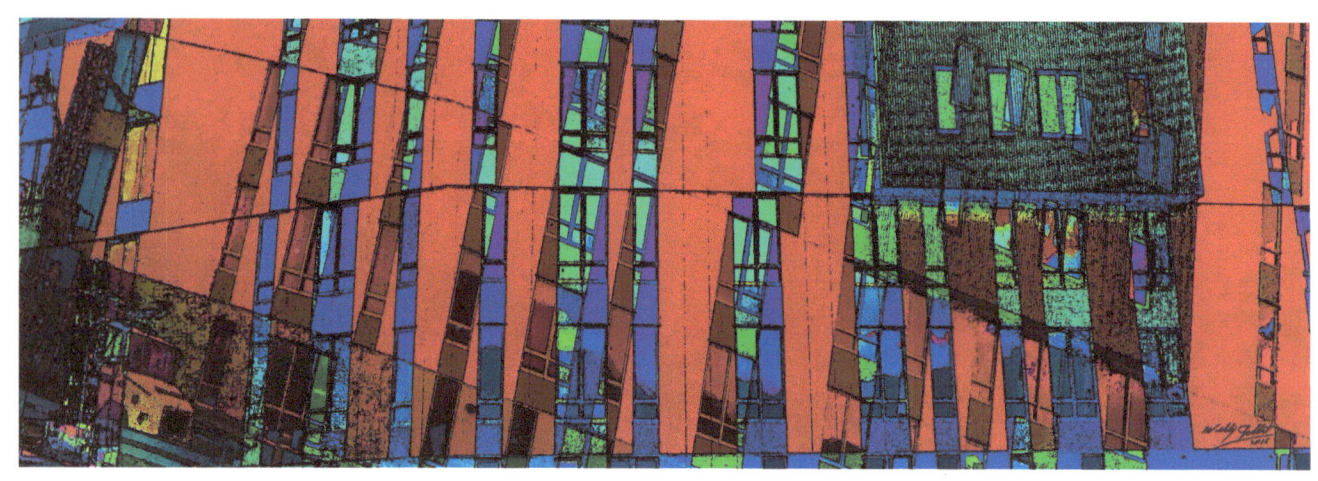

Torn Building #2 – Red

2016, 20" X 60",
Printed on Aluminum, edition of 5

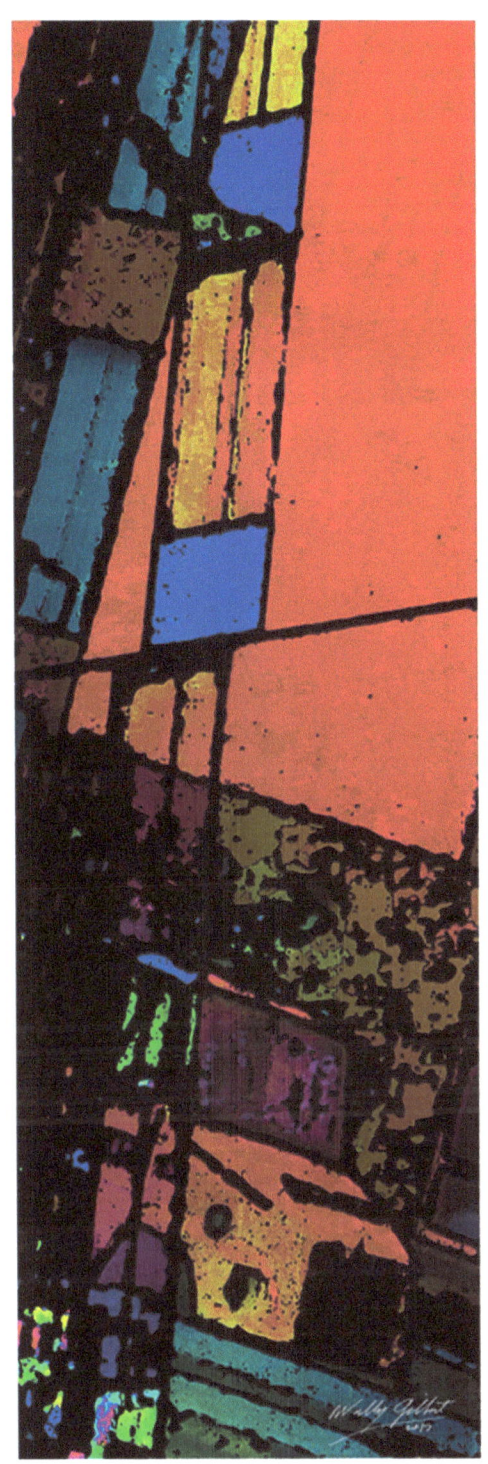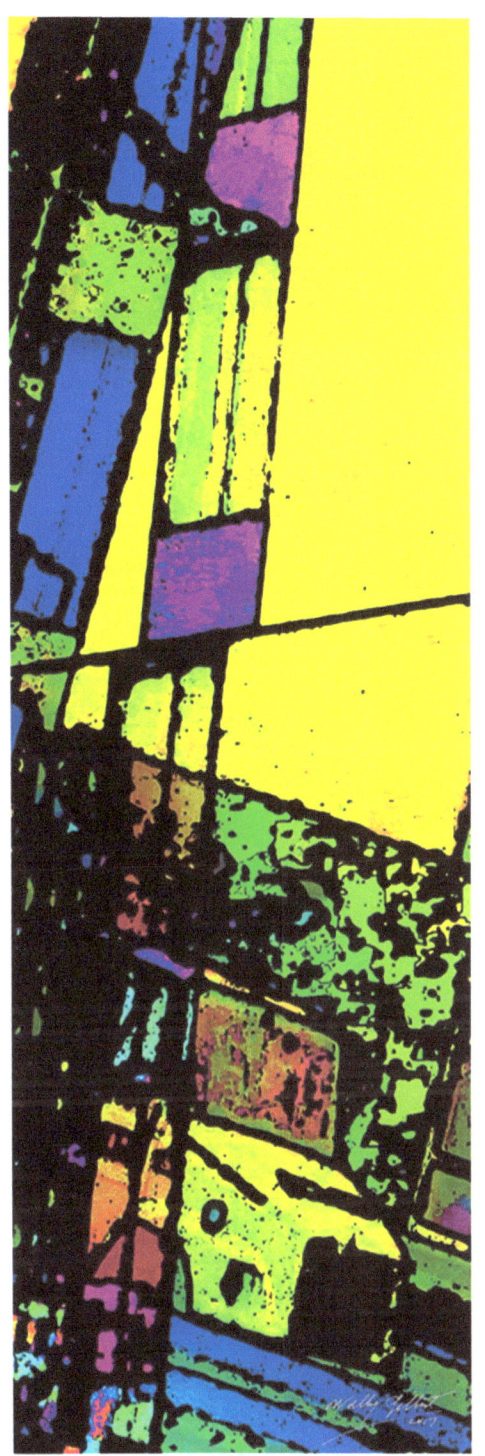

Old Car Diptych

2016, Two Panels, each 36" x 12",
Printed on Aluminum, edition of 5

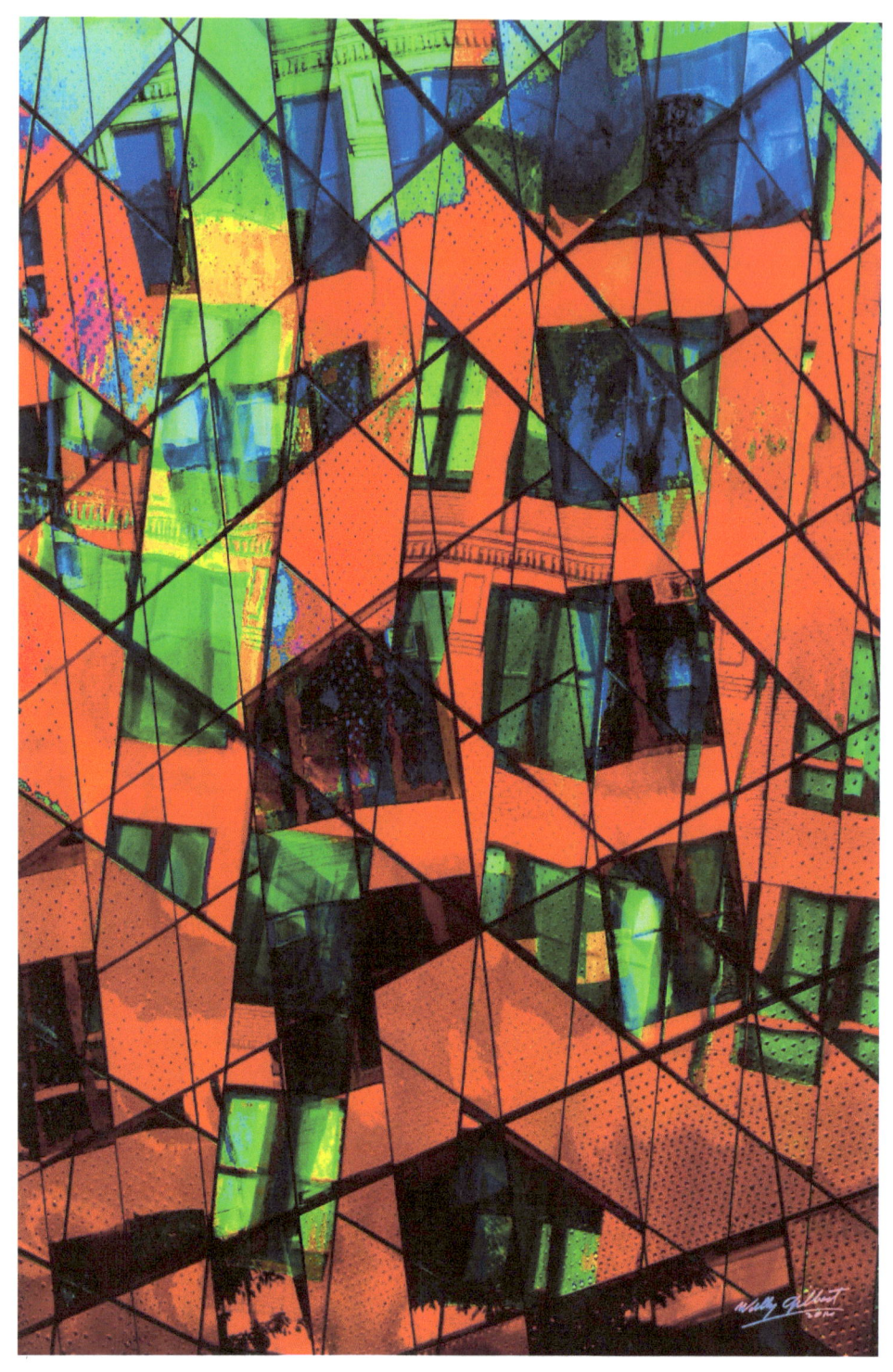

Broken City

2014, 36" x 24",
Printed on Aluminum, edition of 5

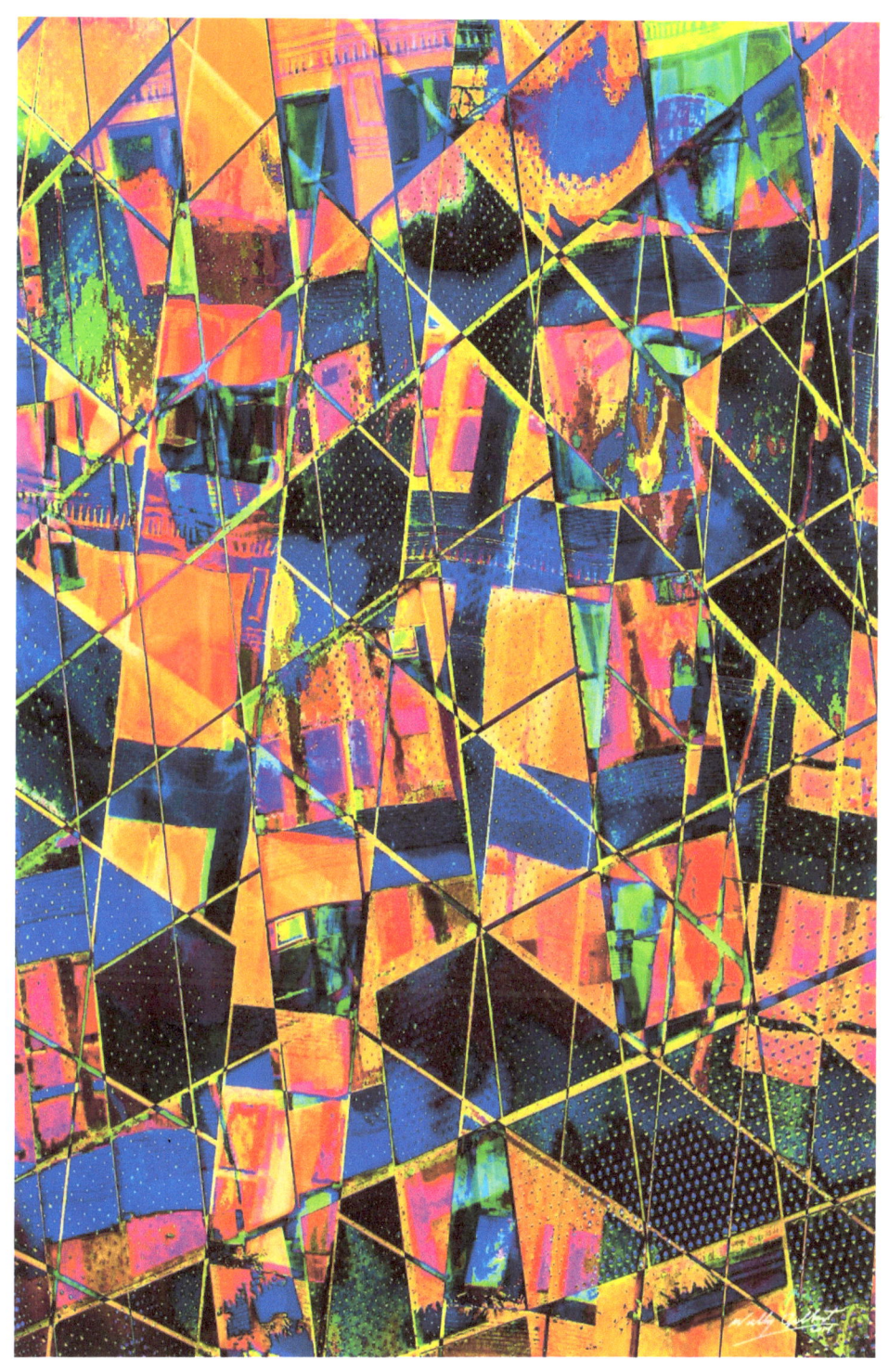

Broken City #II

2014, 36" x 24",
Printed on Aluminum, edition of 5

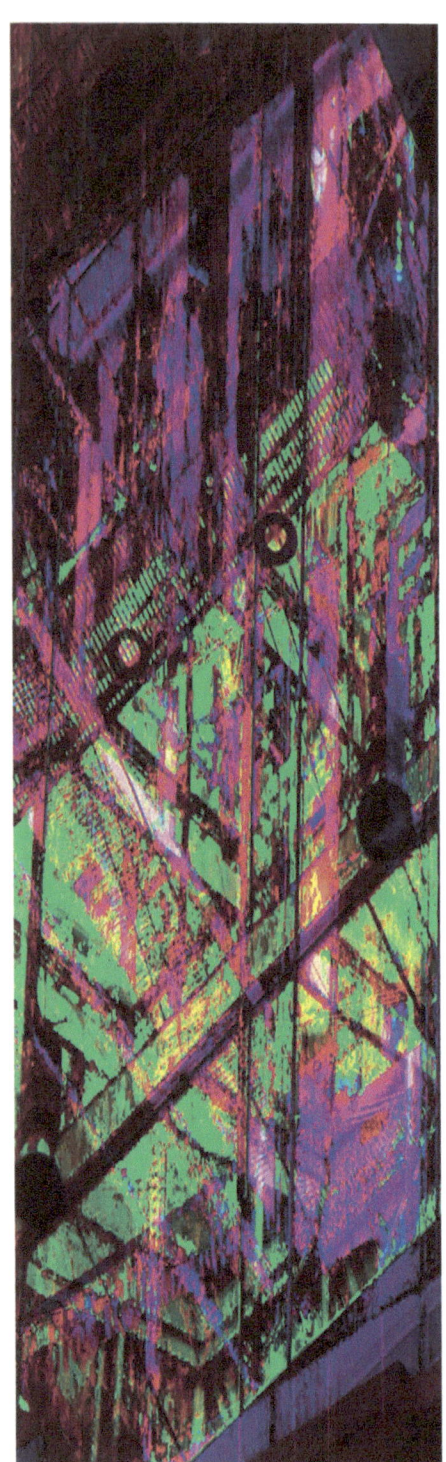 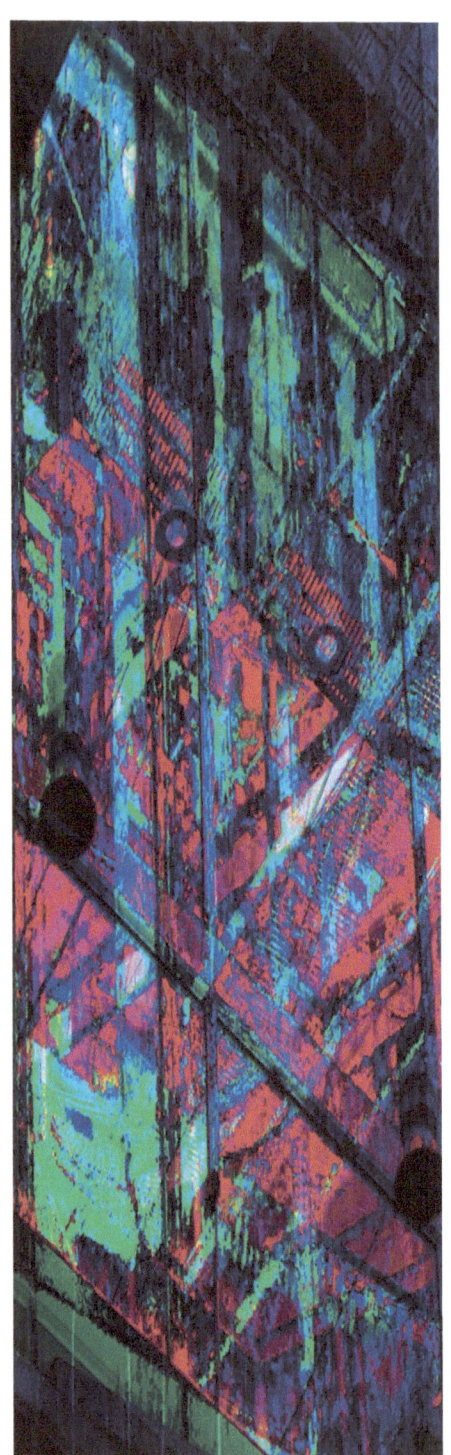

Multiply Diptych

2016, Two Panels, each 36" x 12",
Printed on Aluminum, edition of 5

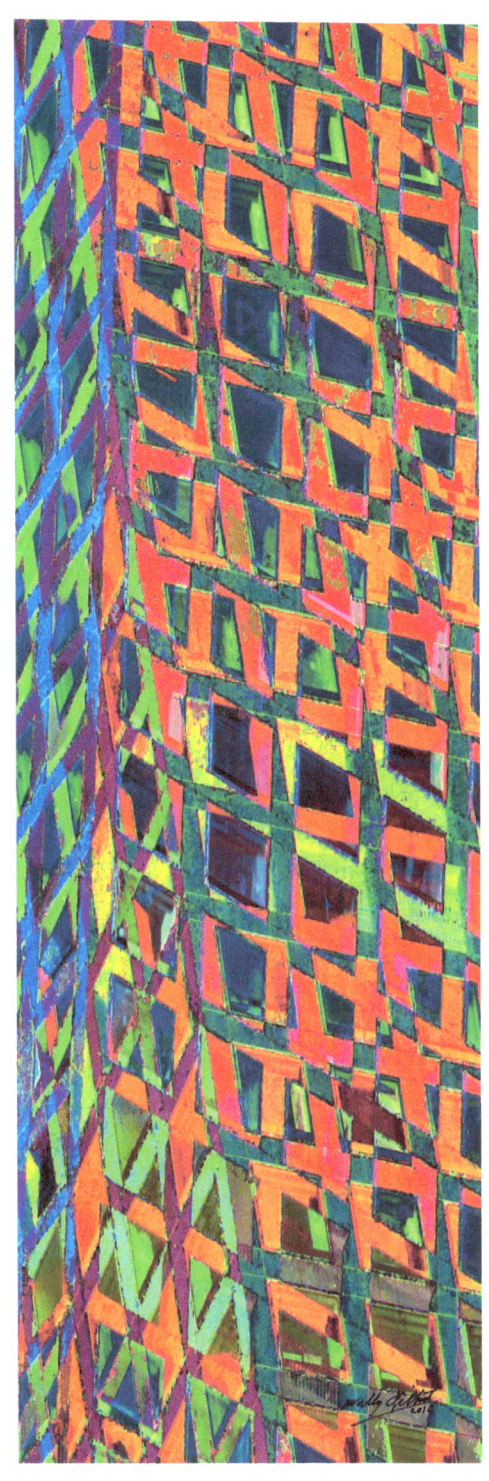

Tall Red

2016, 36" x 12",
Printed on Aluminum, edition of 5

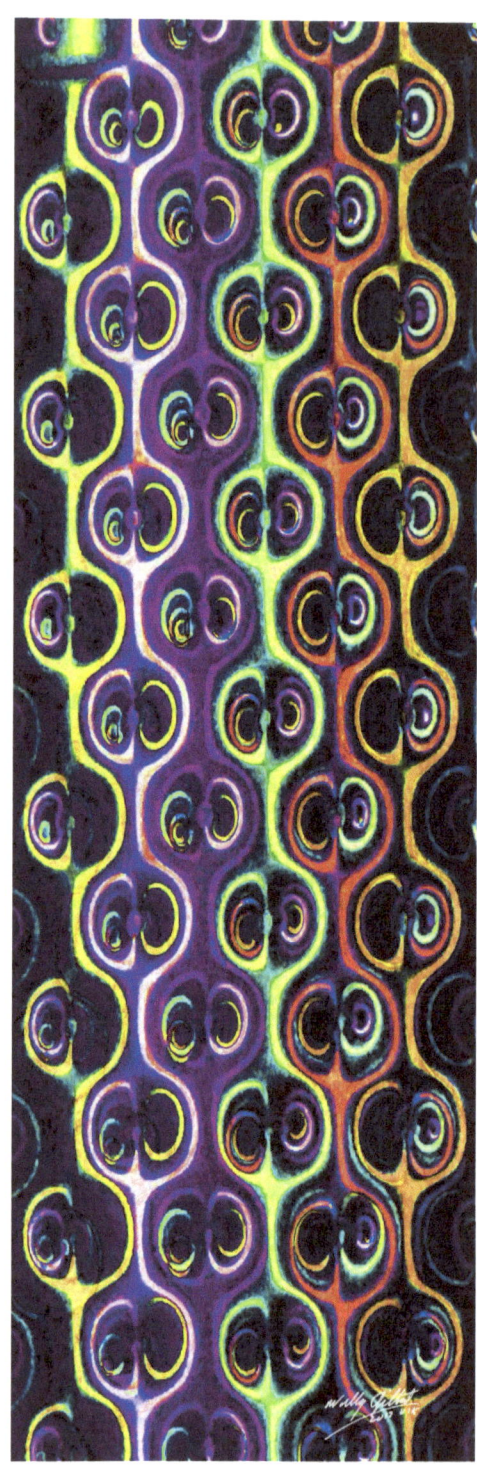

Bewildered

2017, 36" x 12",
Printed on Aluminum, edition of 5

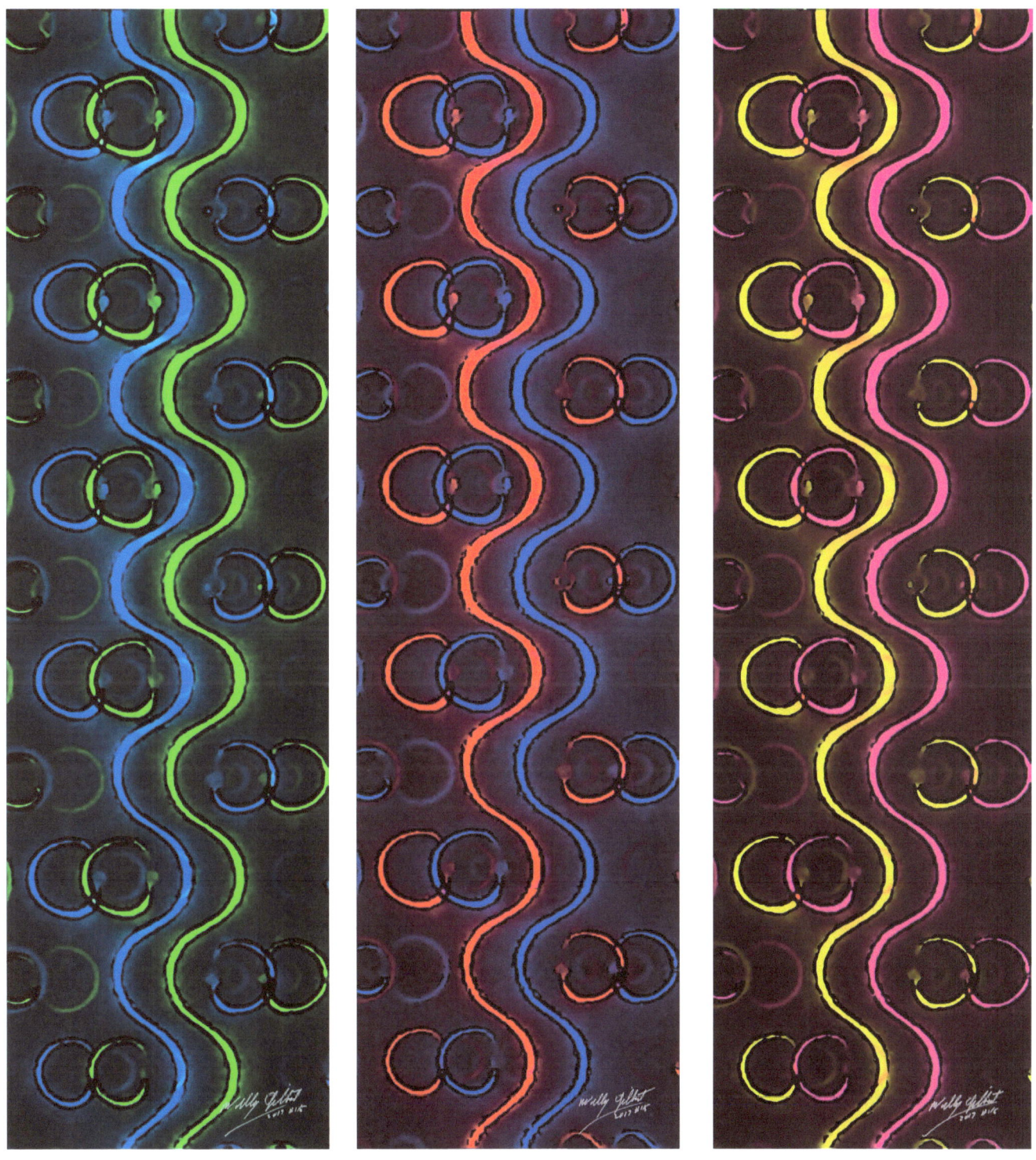

Wiggle Triptych

2017, Three Panels, each 36" x 12",
Printed on Aluminum, edition of 5

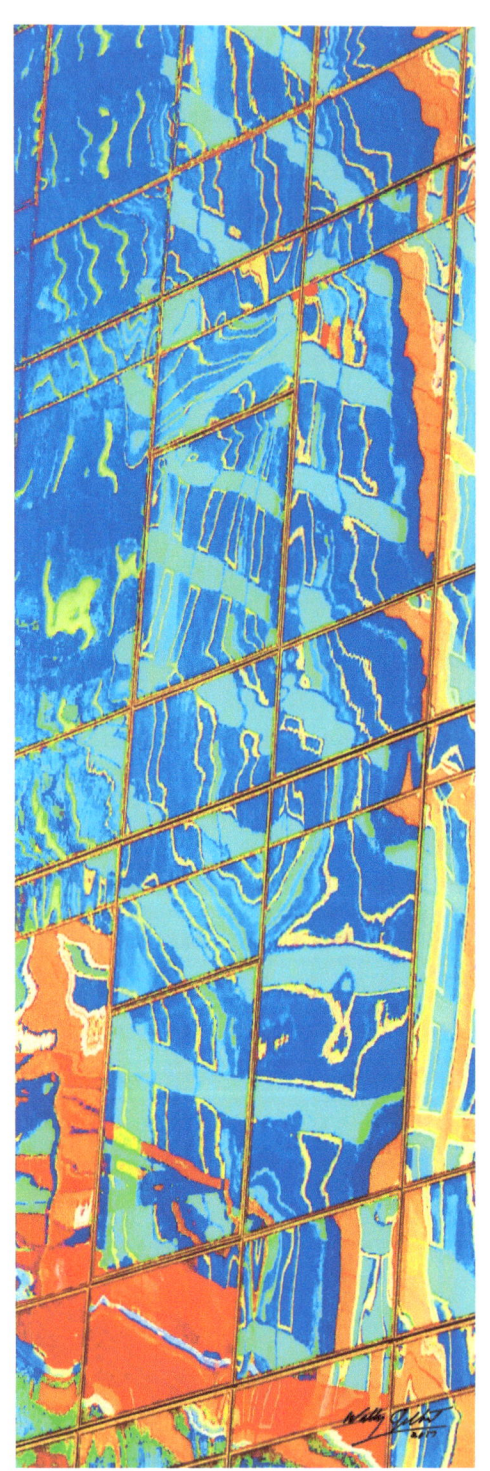 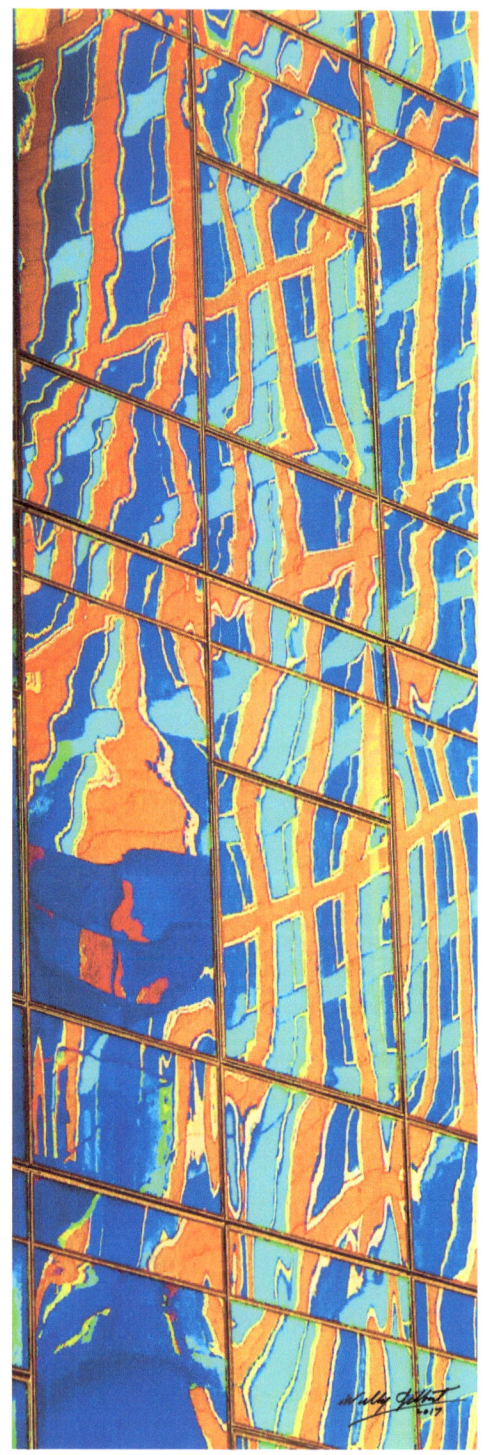

Windows Diptych #1

2017, Two Panels, each 36" x 12",
Printed on Aluminum, edition of 5

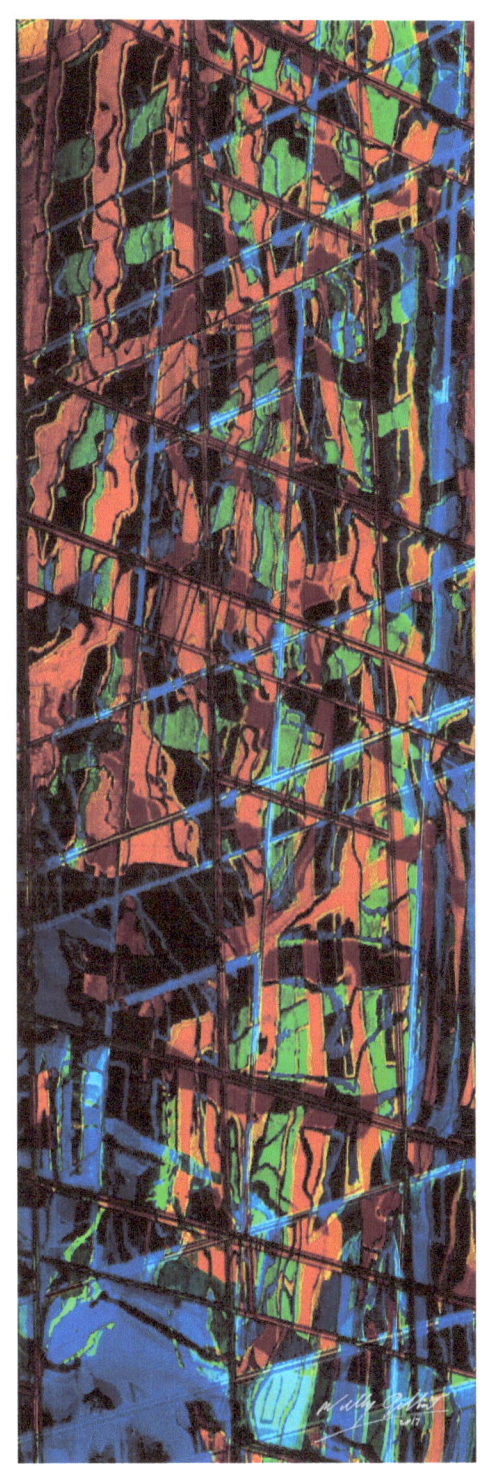 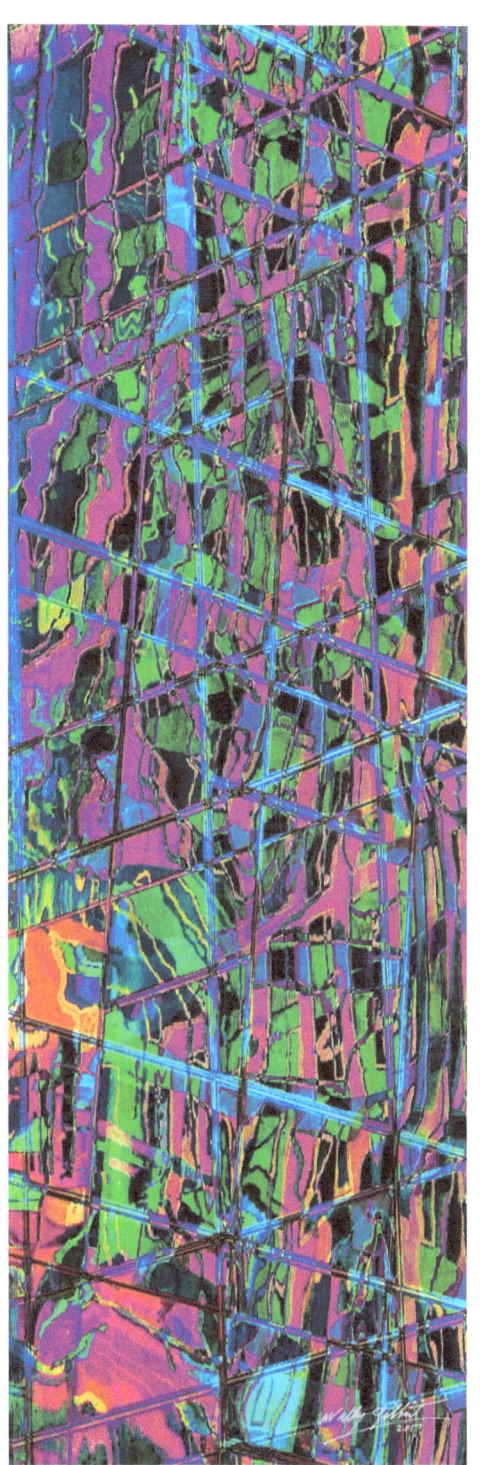

Windows Diptych #2

2017, Two Panels, each 36" x 12",
Printed on Aluminum, edition of 5

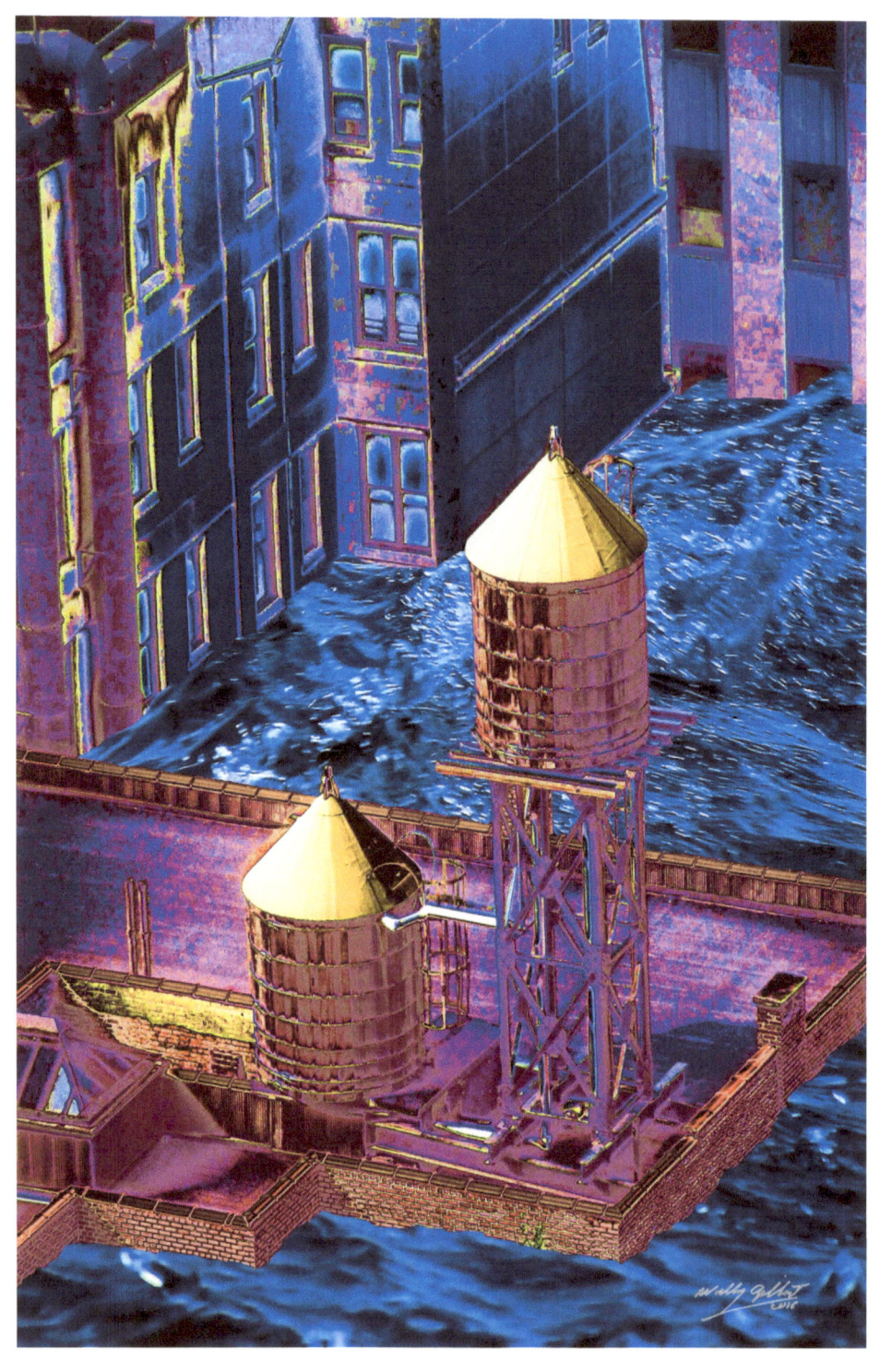

High Water – New York

2016, 36" x 24",
Printed on Aluminum, edition of 5

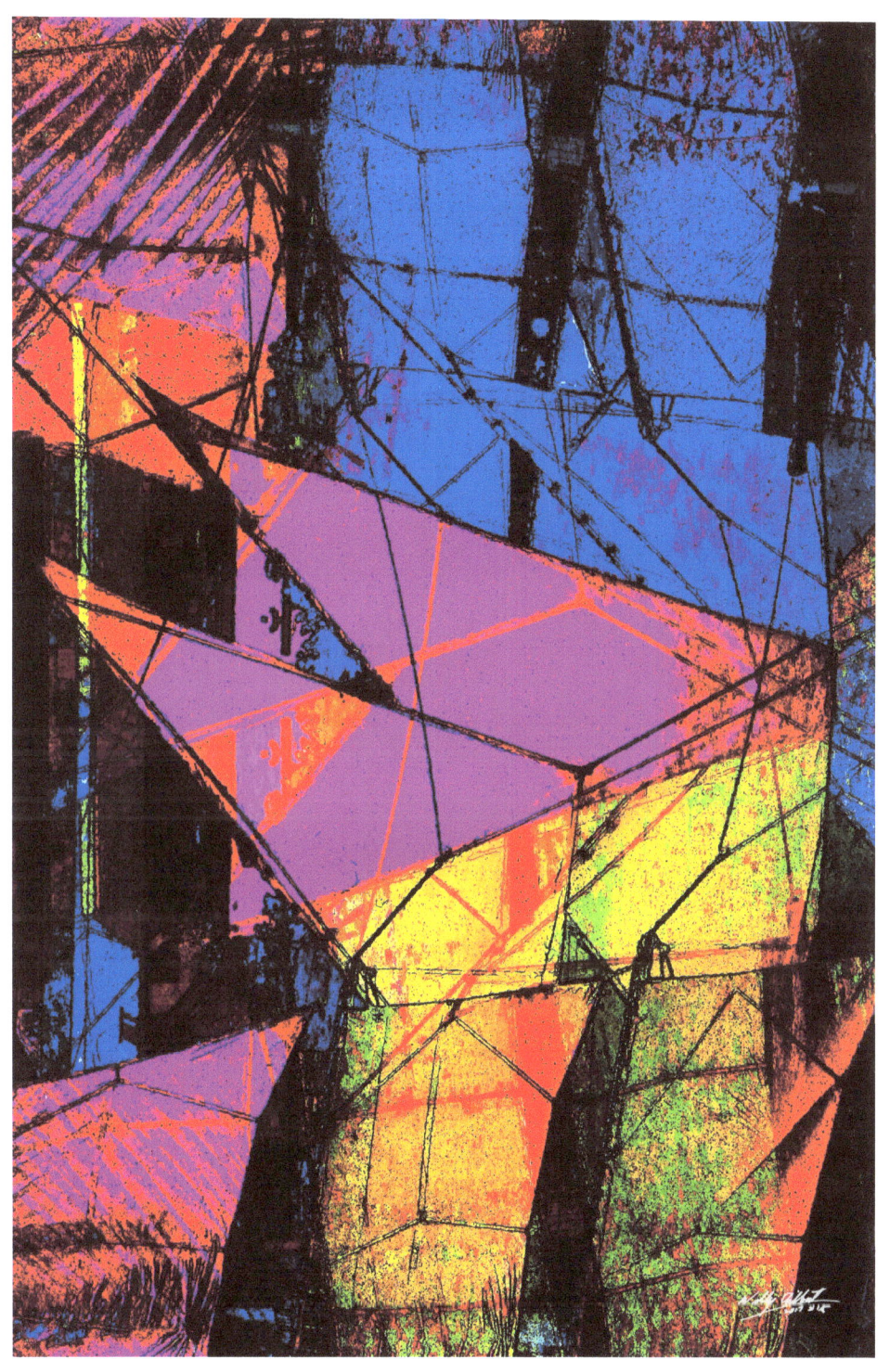

Torment

2017, 36" x 24",
Printed on Aluminum, edition of 5

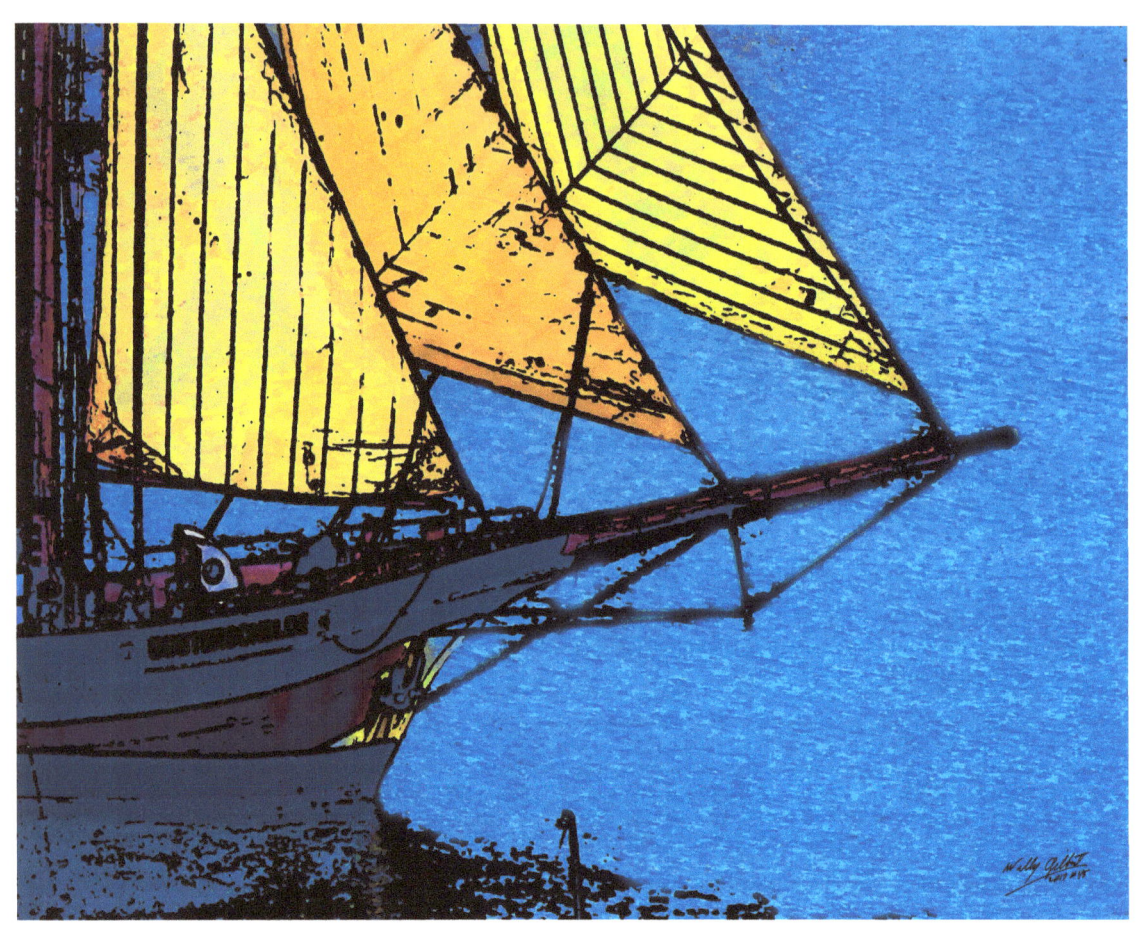

Sails

2017, 24" x 36",
Printed on Aluminum, edition of 5

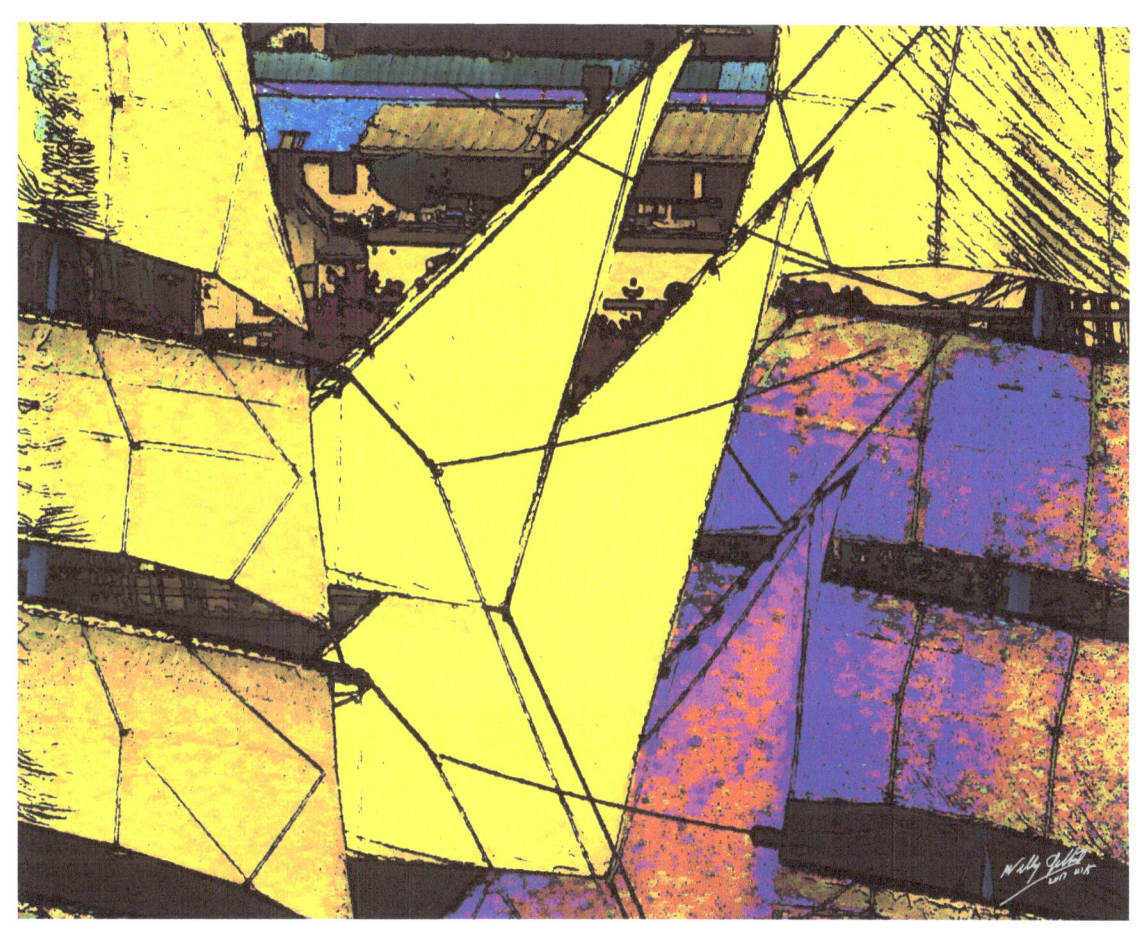

Sails #2 - Yellow

2017, 24" x 36",
Printed on Aluminum, edition of 5

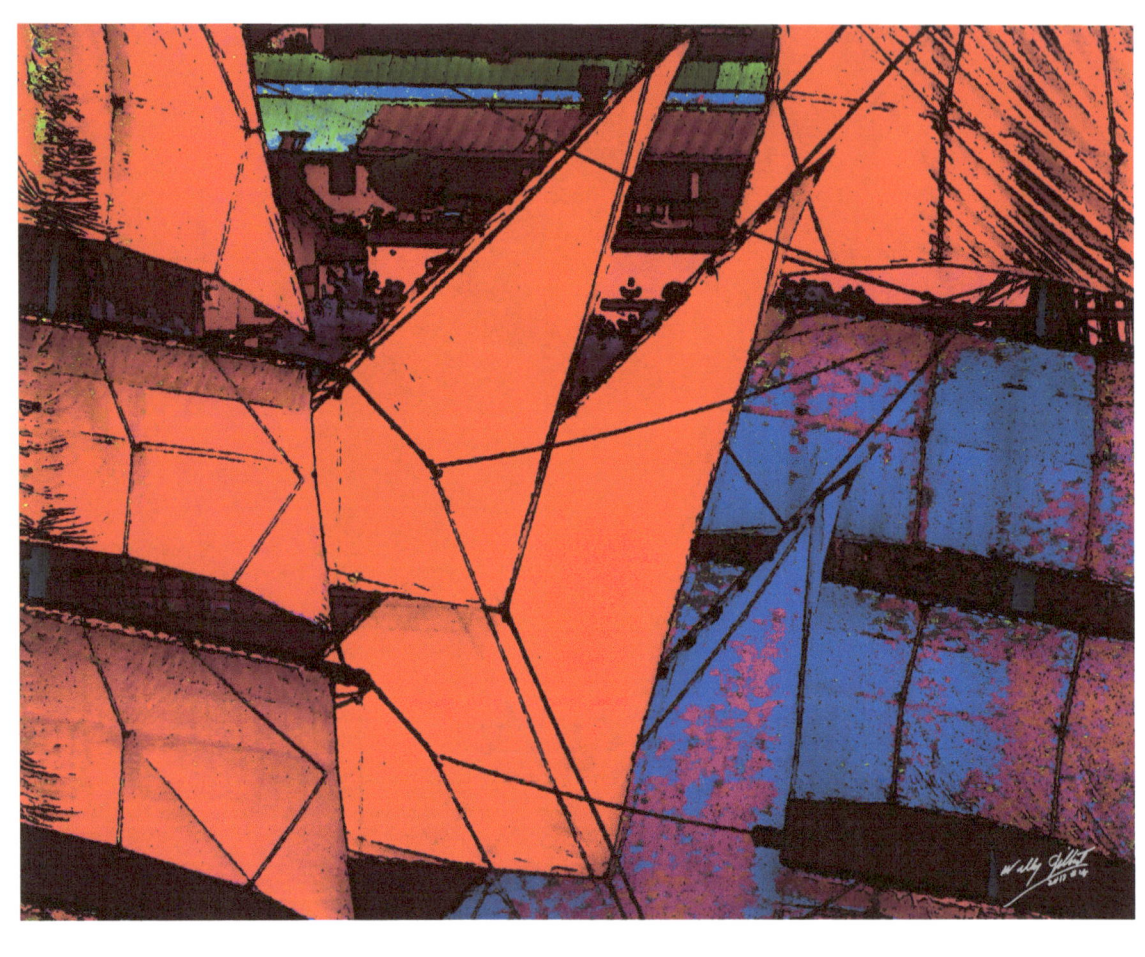

Sails #2 - Red

2017, 24" x 36",
Printed on Aluminum, edition of 5

Wally Gilbert's Statement

I began making digital images as art when I discovered that I could make large prints from images taken with a small digital camera and that these prints carried an emotional and asthetic impact. My earliest work was of fragments of the visual world, either portions of natural scenes or of man's architectural or industrial artifacts. My first one-person show included a 48" x 72" image made from a two mega-pixel camera.

I was invited to Poland, to do an installation at the Norblin Site in Warsaw, by Jan Kubasiewicz and Josef Piwkowski. These photographs of decaying machinery were installed in Warsaw in the Summer of 2007 as twenty-six 12' x 8' hangings and thirty 36" x 24" prints, face-mounted on plexiglas. This show was exhibited again in Lodz and in Poznan.

After photographing dancers in the ballet, I went on to explore abstractions, first in a "Vanishing" series, that was based on a natural form, the outline of a human head. The many patterns produced in that series all shared some aspect of a biological or natural curve, which still was manifest even in the smallest cropping of those images.

In my later work the basic element was a straight, shaded line, which I used to create geometric patterns. The "Geometric Series" explored patterns in color or black-and-white created from overlapping squares or triangles or just from lines, taken either simply or in intersecting groups.

I make many images by hand on the computer. The computer simply holds the intermediate forms as I superpose the many layers I create to build up the image. The images begin in black and white, and then I color them in the computer. I generate these colors either by accessing the colors available or, in a more complicated fashion, by using the ability to change the global input-output functions for each color and intensity separately. When the layers containing the colored images interact with each other, still more color patterns appear. The computer is a digital workspace, driven by my hand and eye.

My most recent work involves photographs moved to extreme values in color space yielding strange color contrasts further superimposed on eachother. These images exemplify my delight in light and form, and my search for a three-dimensional effect on a two-dimensional surface. I search for depth beyond the picture plane and for mystery.

Wally Gilbert's Biography

Wally Gilbert had a long international career as a scientist, working in Molecular Biology on genes and DNA. He was awarded a Nobel Prize in Chemistry, in 1980, for solving the mystery of DNA sequencing. Fred Sanger in England and Gilbert in the United States shared that prize for finding ways to decipher the order of chemical groups along the DNA molecule and hence to make it possible for the first time to read the genes. Those discoveries drove the development of Biology as a gene-based science across the last four decades and led to the working out of the Human Genome program and the current understanding of all organisms.

For the last fifteen years Gilbert has been working in Digital Art. He began by making large images of fragments of the world, focusing on form, texture, and color, using a small digital camera. Very often these pictures were drawn from machines or from architecture. Jan Kubasiewicz, a professor at the Massachusetts College of Art, saw his work and organized his first one-person exhibition in 2004. He was invited to Poland, by Kubasiewicz and Jozef Zuk Piwkowski, to create an installation at the Norblin Site in Warsaw, an old decaying factory. This installation, consisting of twenty-six 12' by 8' hangings and thirty 36" x 24" prints face-mounted on Plexiglas, was installed at Norblin in Warsaw for two months in 2007 and then later that year in Łodz and again in Poznan in 2009. The set of thirty face-mounted prints were also exhibited in New York, Washington D.C., Los Angeles, and San Diego.

Gilbert was invited to participate in creating a book on the Boston Ballet Company. He spent several years photographing ballet dancers in rehearsal. These pictures, which capture the joy and motion of the dancers, appeared in a book on that company "Behind the Scenes at Boston Ballet" by Christine Temin with 68 pictures by Wally Gilbert.

Gilbert then moved to abstractions, first based on silhouettes derived from photographs, then to ever more abstract images based on the human head, at first still interpretable, but then in patterns having only a slight, residual aspect of a biological curve. Then he created digital images, made by hand on the computer, based on geometrical forms. This work involved patterns of superimposed shrinking squares and triangles, strongly colored or in black and white, and led finally to images involving single lines. More recently he has been exploring abstractions created by superimposing several photographic images.

Wally Gilbert — Selected Solo Exhibitions

"Doors to Nowhere,' Salon R, Cambridge, MA	2017
"Broken City," Khaki Gallery, Boston, MA	2016
"Journeying," Permanent exhibition, AGH University, Krakow, Poland	2016--
"Broken City" Viridian Gallery, Chelsea, NYC	2016
"Patterns & Recognition," Seoul National University Bundang Hospital, curated by Chang and Jae Kim	2015-2016
"Transformations," Viridian Artists, Chelsea, NYC	2014
"Patterns & Recognition," The Howard Hughes Medical Institure, Janelia Farm, VA	2014
"Wally Gilbert," CJ Gallery, Art San Diego 2013, San Diego, CA	2013
"Wally Gilbert: A Room of Light," Milton Art Museum, Canton, MA	2013
"Wally Gilbert: Black & White," Khaki Gallery, Boston, MA	2013
"Digital Constellations," Lindau City Museum, Lindau, Germany	2013
"Wally Gilbert: New Black and White Images," Viridian Artists, Chelsea, NYC	2013
"Wally Gilbert", CJ Gallery, Art San Diego 2012, San Diego, CA	2012
"En-Lighten," Khaki Gallery, Boston, MA	2012
"Journeying," The Artemis Gallery, Krakow, Poland, curated by Wieslawa Piotrowska-Sowadska	2012
"Pattern & Recognition," The Art Gallery, Antelope Valley College, Lancaster, CA	2012
"Squares, Triangles, and Lines," Galerie im Einstein, Berlin	2011
"Projekt Norblin," New Art Wet Music Foundation, Bydgoszcz, Poland	2011
"Squares and Triangles," Viridian Artists, Chelsea, NYC	2011
"Vanishing," CJ Gallery, San Diego, CA	2010
"Vanishing Profiles," Khaki Gallery, Boston, MA	2010
"The Norblin Project and Other Images," CJ Gallery and OCIO DESIGN GROUP, San Diego,CA	2010
"Wally@Wainwright," Wainwright Bank, Cambridge, MA	2010
"Vanishing," BAAK Gallery, Cambridge, MA	2009
Norblin Installation, Poznan, Poland, curated by Jan Kubasiewicz and Zuk Piwkowski	2009
"The Norblin Project and other Images," CJ Art Gallery, San Diego, CA	2009
"IN COLOR & BEYOND," Khaki Gallery, Boston, MA	2009
"Fresh Fruit," Mayyim Hayyim Gallery, Newton, MA	2009
"Stillness and Motion," Viridian Artists, Chelsea, NYC	2008
"LEEKS & CHAINS," Khaki Gallery, Wellesley, MA	2008
"The Norblin Project and other Images," CJ Art Gallery, San Diego, CA	2007
BAAK Gallery, Cambridge, MA	2007
Norblin Installation, Galeria PATIO,Lodz, Poland, curated by Zuk Piwkowski, Jan Kubasiewicz, and Aurelia Mandziuk	2007
Norblin Site Installation, Warsaw, Poland, curated by Jan Kubasiewicz and Zuk Piwkowski	2007
"The Norblin Project: Images of Decay," American Center for Physics, College Park, MD	2007
"IN COLOR," Khaki Gallery, Wellesley, MA	2007
"The Norblin Project: Images of Decay," LACDA, Los Angeles, CA	2006
"The Norblin Project: Images of Decay," Viridian Artists, Chelsea, NYC	2006
Jock Colville Hall, Churchill College, University of Cambridge, Cambridge, UK	2006
Ann Janss Gallery, Los Angeles, CA	2005
Doran Gallery, Massachusetts College of Art, Boston, MA, curated by Jan Kubasiewicz	2004

Wally Gilbert Websites

http://wallygilbert.com
http://wallygilbertscarves.com

www.ingramcontent.com/pod-product-compliance
Lightning Source LLC
Chambersburg PA
CBHW051819210526
45473CB00005B/1669